SECRET SIGNS

by James Bow

Crabtree Publishing Company
www.crabtreebooks.com

Crabtree Publishing Company

www.crabtreebooks.com

Author: James Bow
Project Coordinator: Kathy Middleton
Editors: Adrianna Morganelli, Tim Cooke
Proofreader: Crystal Sikkens
Designer: Lynne Lennon
Cover Design: Margaret Amy Salter
Picture Researcher: Andrew Webb
Picture Manager: Sophie Mortimer
Art Director: Jeni Child
Editorial Director: Lindsey Lowe
Children's Publisher: Anne O'Daly
Production Coordinator and
    Prepress Technician: Samara Parent
Print Coordinator: Katherine Berti

Photographs
Cover: **Getty Images** (background); **Shutterstock** (middle)
Interior: **Alamy:** David Cairns 11, Robert Harding
Picture Library 13; **Getty Images:** AFP/Stringer 28;
istockphoto: 24; **Kobal Collection:** Global Hdtv 29;
NASA: GRIN 4; **NSA:** 6; **Public Domain:** 26, 27; **Robert
Hunt Library:** 7, 8, 17; **Shutterstock:** 5, 10, 15, 21,
Steven Belanger 25, Zbynek Burival 14, Elena Eisseeva
20, Matthew Jaques 16-17, Pecold 18, 19, Gary Yim 12;
Thinkstock: Digital Vision 22, istockphoto 9, 23.

Library and Archives Canada Cataloguing in Publication

Bow, James, 1972-
    Secret signs / James Bow.

(Mystery files)
Includes index.
Issued also in electronic formats.
ISBN 978-0-7787-1125-4 (bound).--ISBN 978-0-7787-1129-2 (pbk.)

    1. Cryptography--Juvenile literature. 2. Ciphers--Juvenile
literature. 3. Signs and symbols--Juvenile literature. I. Title. II. Series:
Mystery files (St. Catharines, Ont.)

Z103.3.B68 2013   j652'.8   C2012-908509-X

Library of Congress Cataloging-in-Publication Data

Bow, James.
 Secret signs / James Bow.
    pages cm. -- (Mystery files)
 Includes index.
 ISBN 978-0-7787-1125-4 (reinforced library binding : alk. paper) -
- ISBN 978-0-7787-1129-2 (pbk. : alk. paper) -- ISBN (invalid)
978-1-4271-9277-6 (electronic pdf) -- ISBN 978-1-4271-9201-1
(electronic html)
 1. Symbolism--Juvenile literature. 2. Signs and symbols--Juvenile
literature. I. Title.

 CB475.B69 2013
 302.2'223--dc23
                     2012049883

Crabtree Publishing Company
www.crabtreebooks.com   1-800-387-7650

Published in Canada
Crabtree Publishing
616 Welland Ave.
St. Catharines, ON
L2M 5V6

Published in the United States
Crabtree Publishing
PMB 59051
350 Fifth Avenue, 59th Floor
New York, New York 10118

Published by **CRABTREE PUBLISHING COMPANY in 2013**
Copyright © 2013 Brown Bear Books Ltd

Printed in Canada/012013/MA20121217

Contents

Introduction

Words and images exist for us to send messages to other people. But what if you want to send a secret message that only a few people can understand? That is when we use hidden signs.

Keeping Secrets

To pass secret messages, we use codes and **ciphers**. A code is any way of disguising a meaning. A cipher is a form of code, in which the letters in a message are replaced with other letters or **symbols**. Other hidden messages do not use words.

The signs on this disk are designed for aliens to read.

Do some old carvings contain secret symbols?

They may take the form of ancient stones or of giant figures carved in the ground. Perhaps the messages are so old their original meanings have been lost. Sometimes they are so mysterious, people look for signs that are not even there.

Human-made symbols will soon leave the solar system. In 1977, spaceships were sent into space carrying **audio** disks. The disks have pictures on them that scientists hope will show aliens how to play them and where they can find us.

In this book, you will look for hidden signs. You will explore mysterious organizations and visit ancient sites. You will learn their secrets—and you can ask yourself, "What does it all mean?"

Mystery words...

audio: related to hearing

Writing in CODES

The use of codes and ciphers goes back to ancient times. The oldest known code was written in Iraq in about 1500 B.C. A code is any kind of secret message. In a cipher, the actual letters are replaced by other letters or symbols.

The Spartan army of ancient Greece used ciphers. Soldiers wound a strip of parchment around a cylinder rod called a scytale. A message was written across the paper. When the paper was unwound, the message was scrambled up. The recipient of the message wound it around his own scytale to read it.

A strip of letters wrapped around a scytale contains a message.

Modern Ciphers

The military still use ciphers. In World War II, the Germans used an Enigma machine to **encrypt** messages. Mathematicians like Marian Rejewski and Alan Turing worked hard to break the codes. The machines they built to help them were the first modern computers.

Today, the military, governments, and banks are all working to make codes unbreakable. They keep updating their codes to stay ahead of the codebreakers.

The Enigma machine used gears and rotors to encode messages.

Mystery words...

encrypt: to turn a message into code

Secret BROTHERS

Sometimes a love of secrets takes on a life of its own. For example, the Freemasons are seen as a mysterious organization. People dream up **conspiracies** about them, claiming they have a sinister influence on world governments. The Freemasons have a tradition of secrecy, but they are no longer very mysterious.

Mystery words...

conspiracies: secret plots to achieve a particular purpose

In reality, the Freemasons began as a labor union. In the Middle Ages, people who carved stone were known as masons. People paid the masons well for their skills as they built the great cathedrals of Europe. The masons protected the secrets of their trade from outsiders. Perhaps because of their connection with the important religious buildings, those secrets became **rituals**. Many masons became rich. They looked after other members of the group.

Masonic tools are used in this stamp of the Freemason's crest.

Mystery File:
SECRET GESTURES

Masons identify each other with a famous secret handshake. You clasp the hand of a fellow Mason and touch the tops of your fingers against his wrist. There are other "secret" gestures in freemasonry, but today most can be seen on the Internet.

Modern Masons

Today, the Freemasons are a social club. There are more than six million members, most of whom know nothing about cutting stone. The mason's customs and tools are now seen as symbols about how to live a good life. A lot of their work goes toward raising money for charity.

Chapel of SIGNS

Rosslyn Chapel was built in 1496 near the village of Roslin in Scotland. Some people believe the chapel is full of hidden signs linking it to a mysterious organization known as the Knights Templar, and so to the Holy Grail.

Rosslyn Chapel is full of carvings.

The Knights Templar were Catholics who fought in Crusades, or holy wars, in the Christian Holy Land in Jerusalem in the 12th and 13th centuries. Some people said the knights took relics home from the Holy Land. The relics included the Holy Grail, the cup Jesus is said to have used at the **Last Supper**. Some people believe the chapel contains clues to where the treasures are hidden: perhaps within the **crypt** of the chapel itself.

Mystery words...

crypt: an underground chamber beneath a church

A False Trail

It is a good story; but in fact, the chapel was not built until 185 years after the Templar **order** ended. The family who built it was actually an enemy of the Templars. Most historians do not believe the chapel contains any Templar symbols—but that does not prevent tourists from trying to uncover its secrets.

Rosslyn Chapel attracts many visitors to study its "symbols."

Mystery File: DA VINCI CODE

Dan Brown's hit 2003 novel *The Da Vinci Code* stressed Rosslyn Chapel's supposed connection to the Knights Templar. The book inspired a tourist boom. But many scholars dispute the historical facts on which the book claims to be based.

Mystery LINES

In the Nazca Desert of Peru, shallow lines seem to have been scratched in the dirt. On the ground, they look like random marks. Only when the lines are seen from the air do they appear to be huge drawings.

The drawings included birds, mammals, and even a man in what looked like a spacesuit. The drawings could not be seen clearly from the ground. Some people argued that they must have been made to be seen from

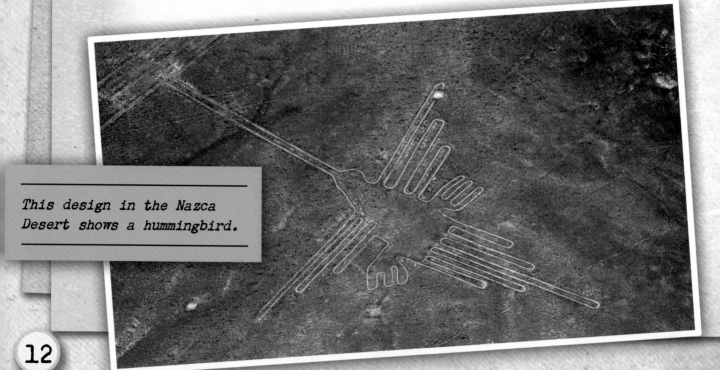

This design in the Nazca Desert shows a hummingbird.

the air—but centuries before humans invented flight. Were their creators sending messages to visitors from the sky or even to aliens?

Lost Meaning

In reality, the pictures *can* be seen from the ground, from nearby hills. But that doesn't take away the mystery of the symbols. When they were made between about 400 and 650 A.D., their creators intended them to have some meaning. Sadly, today that meaning remains a mystery.

Mystery File:
HILL FIGURES

The Nazca Desert isn't the only place in the world with drawings on the ground. In England, figures were carved by ancient peoples who cut into the turf to reveal the white chalk rock beneath. No one knows the meaning of such giant figures.

Mystery words...

turf: the top level of soil, which is held together by grass roots

Codes of the PHARAOHS

In 2560 B.C., the Egyptian pharaoh Khufu ordered that his tomb be built as a giant stone pyramid 480 feet (146 m) tall. Khufu wanted to make sure that people thousands of years later would know where he was buried.

Many people believe that the pyramids also hid many more messages. They were positioned, for example, so that their corners pointed to holy places. Within the pyramids were hidden signs that acted as **curses** to guard the tomb. And inside the coffins were paintings known as the Books of the Dead. Their job was

The pharaohs were buried with many symbols of their power.

Mystery words...

curses: magic spells that cause harm to someone

to tell the spirit of the dead person how to get to the afterlife, where the Egyptians believed the dead could live on.

Pyramid Symbols

Even the shape of the pyramid had a message. Archaeologists think it represented the first land rising from the waters at the beginning of the world. The shape also represents the descending rays of the Sun. So far, 138 pyramids have been found in Egypt—and each seems to have its own secrets.

Do the pyramids hold secrets that we have yet to learn?

STONEHENGE

The great stones tower over the plain around them. Stonehenge—the "stone circle"—was built about 5,000 years ago in southern Britain.

Stonehenge was clearly important. Some of the huge stones came from many miles away, and moving them would have taken a huge amount of work by the whole community. But what purpose inspired such an effort?

Stone Calendar

In its final shape, Stonehenge was a circle of stones joined by a **lintel**. It surrounded a ring of smaller stone pillars and a horseshoe of large stones. It was positioned so that the first rays of the midsummer sunrise and the last rays of the midwinter sunset shone into the center of the **monument**. Some archaeologists believe that the monument was a calendar for predicting the changing of the seasons. That was vital knowledge for farmers who needed to know when to plant or harvest their crops.

This mural recreates Stonehenge in about 3000 B.C.

Today, many of the original stones have fallen down.

Mystery File: DRUID MONUMENT

Many people think Stonehenge is linked to ancient Celtic priests called Druids. That link was first made in the 17th century, but it is mistaken. The Celts arrived in Britain approximately 3,000 years after Stonehenge was begun.

Mystery words...

lintel: a horizontal crosspiece, often used above a doorway

Passage for the SUN

Do the carvings at Newgrange hide a message?

At around the same time as Stonehenge was begun in Britain in 3000 B.C., work began on a tomb in Ireland. Like Stonehenge, Newgrange was built to face the rising Sun.

On the winter **solstice**, the shortest day of the year, light from the sunrise floods into a special opening called a roof box. It follows a long passageway and penetrates into the very heart of the tomb, where it fills the central chamber with light for 17 minutes.

Perhaps those who built the tomb were trying to "capture" the Sun on the shortest day of the year. That might help ensure that the days would get longer again as the year went on. Or perhaps the light was for the benefit of whoever was buried in the tomb—but whoever that was is another mystery.

Unlike Stonehenge, Newgrange was only used for a short time before it was sealed up.

TOMB LESSONS

How people are buried reveals a lot about what their society believed. Some dead people were buried with their belongings to take to the next life. Other peoples thought the spirit left the body. They often cremated the bodies of their dead.

The entrance to the tomb is guarded by a carved boulder.

Carvings in the Stone

Newgrange has carvings all over its stones. Most are abstract swirls or rectangles. No one know what the designs mean. Many designs were placed where no one could see them: no one alive, anyway.

Mystery words...

solstice: the name for the longest and shortest days of the year

Silent
SENTINELS

Near the village of Carnac in western France stands a field of huge stones older than Stonehenge. They were built around 3,300 B.C. What were the builders trying to tell us?

The stones are not laid out at random. A total of some 3,100 stones march across the landscape in a series of lines and fans. One group, called the Menec alignment, has 11 rows of stones stretching over half a mile (0.8 km). The Kermario alignment has 1,029 stones in ten columns

Mystery words...

megaliths: large stones that are deliberately placed in arrangements

stretching over 1,400 yards (1,280 m). There are also several burial mounds.

Linked to the Sun?

Archaeologists have various theories about the stones' purpose. Some suggest they may have helped detect earthquakes. Others believe that the stones were aligned with the Sun. That might mean they were a huge calendar, a little like Stonehenge. But Carnac's true message remains another of history's secrets.

Some experts think building with **megaliths** began on the Mediterranean island of Malta. From there, the practice spread up Europe's Atlantic coast. That is why ancient stone monuments often stand near the coasts of France, Britain, and Ireland.

The Carnac stones stretch over the ground in row after row.

Signals in the CORN

In the early 1970s, strange designs began appearing in fields across England. Grass or crops would be flattened to form circles or other shapes that could only be seen from the air. The crop circles became a global media sensation.

The designs can be very complex.

What did the crop circles mean? And who or what was creating them? There was never any sign of other activity in the fields. The circles simply seemed to appear overnight.

Some people looked for a natural explanation. As early as 1686, scientist Robert Plot had studied "fairy rings." These were patches on the ground where grass grew faster than the grass around it.

Mystery words...

media: organizations that report the news

Perhaps the circles were made by winds or tornadoes. Other people pointed out that the designs were too precise and their edges too straight to be natural.

A Confession

In 1991, two men came forward. They claimed to have made most of the early crop circles. They showed how it could be done by using a plank of wood to flatten the crops. The circles had no meaning at all. The more elaborate shapes that followed were the work of other pranksters and artists trying to go one step better.

Mystery File: WALLABY CIRCLES

Crop circles have appeared in Tasmania that are definitely not made by humans. The cause has been identified as wallabies. The animals eat from fields of poppies. The poppies contain drugs that make the wallabies run around in circles.

Canyon of
SECRETS

Chaco Canyon, in New Mexico, is full of reminders of the Pueblo, or Anasazi. These Native Americans lived here between 900 and 1150 A.D. They left behind a landscape full of mysterious hidden signs.

Some Pueblo structures were half-buried in the ground.

At the heart of the canyon are the ruins of community homes. There are also round, sunken structures known as **kivas**. They were used in religious rituals. Radiating out from the middle of the canyon is a whole series of roads. They are very straight and stretch over long distances. Some are very wide. While some of the roads lead to other Pueblo villages, others seem to have no destination and were used very little. One theory is that these were ritual highways rather than real

These Pueblo petroglyphs show hunters and horses.

Mystery File: SUN DAGGERS

On an outcrop named Fajada Butte in Chaco Canyon is a spiral petroglyph. It is positioned so that, on the summer solstice, a dagger of sunlight pierces it. The spiral may have been used so that priests knew when to perform rituals.

roads. They all pointed to the spiritual center of the Pueblo people in the canyon.

Rock Carvings

All over the canyon, the Pueblo carved petroglyphs. These are designs scratched into rock faces that show people, tools, and even the plans of buildings. These drawings have been preserved by the hot, dry conditions.

Banknote of
SYMBOLS

The **U.S.** dollar bill is full of symbols. It features patriotic images, people from history, and even important buildings and animals. But does it also contain hidden messages from the founders of the nation?

One of the most frequent symbols on the bill is the number 13. The 13s represent the 13 colonies that rebelled against the British in the American Revolution. On the back of the bill has two circles. One has an image of a pyramid with 13 steps. The other circle shows an eagle. In the eagle's left foot is 13 arrows. In its right foot is an **olive branch** with 13 leaves and 13 olives. Above the eagle is 13 stars. The dollar bill has other symbols of 13. Can you find the others?

Freemasons' Plot

The pyramid with the floating eye is a symbol of the Freemasons. Some people believe the founders used the symbol to show that Freemasons founded the U.S. government. They fear that Freemasons still secretly control the U.S. government —and other governments around the world. Most experts believe these people are completely wrong about their theory.

Banknotes have complex designs to prevent them from being copied.

Message to the FUTURE

Some signs become messages from history to the present. Recently, the U.S. Department of Energy tried to figure out how to send a message to people thousands of years from now. The message is simple: don't dig here.

This symbol is used today as a warning of radioactivity.

The U.S. government is looking for a place to build a dump to store nuclear waste. The waste would remain dangerously **radioactive** for thousands of years. To get an idea of how long, imagine the amount of time that has passed since the Egyptians built the pyramids. Now imagine that same amount of time from now into the future. The nuclear waste would still be deadly then: but most traces of the civilization that produced it may have disappeared.

Today, we don't know why people built, say, Stonehenge. So, it's likely the reason we dumped nuclear waste won't be remembered in the future, either. How do we tell people then that it is dangerous to dig?

Design Competition

The U.S. Department of Energy held a design competition asking

artists to create warning signs for a world that might have forgotten our forms of language. The designs people came up with included a field of spikes, information recorded in many different languages, and stick-figure images of humans. How would you choose to send a message to the future?

Glossary

audio Related to hearing

cipher A code in which letters are replaced by other letters or symbols

conspiracies Secret plots to achieve a particular purpose

crypt An underground chamber beneath a church

curses Magic spells that cause harm to someone

encrypt To turn a message into code

kivas Semi-buried rooms used for religious rituals

Last Supper According to Christianity is the last meal Jesus had before his death on the cross

lintel A horizontal crosspiece, often used above a doorway

media Organizations that report the news

megaliths Large stones that are deliberately placed in arrangements

monuments Works of art made to remember things from the past

olive branch A branch from an olive tree, symbolizing peace

order A group of knights that follow religious rules, like monks

radioactive Dangerous particles given off by decaying atoms

resistance fighters Armed groups of people that fought against the German occupation in France during World War II

rituals Religious ceremonies that follow a fixed order

solstice The name for the longest and shortest days of the year

symbol Anything that stands for or represents something else

turf The top layer of soil, which is held together by grass roots

Find Out More

BOOKS

Aronson, Marc. *If Stones Could Speak: Unlocking the Secrets of Stonehenge*. National Geographic Children's Books, 2010.

Croy, Anita. *Ancient Pueblo* (National Geographic Investigates). National Geographic Children's Books, 2009.

Langley, Andrew. *Codes and Codebreaking* (Spies and Spying). Smart Apple Media, 2010.

Southwell, Dean, and Sean Twist. *Secret Societies* (Mysteries and Conspiracies). Rosen Central, 2007.

WEBSITES

Stonehenge
A guide to the monument and its history
www.stonehenge.org.uk/

Chaco Canyon
National Park Service guide to the Chaco Culture
www.nps.gov/chcu/index.htm

Freemasonry
The Freemasons' public guide to their signs and symbols
www.masonic-lodge-of-education.com/index.html

Nazca Lines
National Geographic magazine article about the meaning of the lines
http://ngm.nationalgeographic.com/2010/03/nasca/hall-text/2

Index